A Vertical Mile

A
Vertical
Mile

POEMS BY
Richard Wakefield

ABLE MUSE PRESS

Able Muse Press

www.ablemusepress.com

Printed in the United States of America

Library of Congress Control Number: 2011945744

ISBN 978-0-9878705-7-5

Foreword copyright ©2012 by David Sanders

Cover image: *Magic Morning* by Jacqueline Barkla

Cover & book design by Alexander Pepple

Able Muse Press is an imprint of *Able Muse: A Review of Poetry, Prose & Art*—at
www.ablemuse.com

Able Muse Press
467 Saratoga Avenue #602
San Jose, CA 95129

As always and with everything, to CMW, EGW, MCW.

Acknowledgments

Over the past ten years, poems in this collection (sometimes in slightly different form) have appeared in the following publications.

Online and print journals:

Able Muse, Measure, Light Quarterly, The Buckeye, Trillium, The Formalist, Iambs & Trochees, Modern Age, The Comstock Review.

Anthologies:

Pacific Rim Poets, Many Paths to the Summit, In the Shadow of Tahoma.

Foreword

To borrow a phrase from Robert Frost, Richard Wakefield gives us "a poetry that talks." Not only does he speak in our modern vernacular; he has something to say, and he ranges widely in saying it. Wakefield knows the city and the country. He knows farming, with its uncertainties and heartbreak. He knows technology and its trade-offs. As the volume's title suggests, he knows mountains and the forces that shape them, the rivers that flow from them. He knows animals, domestic and wild. He takes us into geology, biology, history, astronomy. And most of all, Wakefield knows people.

Wakefield crafts his verse to exacting standards yet keeps it uncontrived. Each sentence traces an unhurried arc, moving to his rhymes or through them to complete its idea, as we see in the final poem of the collection, aptly named "Terminus." Its speaker has followed a mountain stream to its source, and as he sees a dying salmon fertilize eggs in the snow-melt pool where both the stream and fish have arisen, he brings together various ends and beginnings in a world where nothing truly begins or ends. Like the hikers who "gasp in mountain air" from their strenuous climb and whose "pulses pound like lovers' in the clinch," the spent salmon, in its procreative task, "flops and writhes" as its "gill slits stir up rapid clouds of silt." We watch in slow motion as "silver fades to gray/ and disappears beneath a pall of milt," and a final sentence reminds us of the transitory nature of everything, including the transpiring lives through which we see:

> The mountain sun has been so hot today
>
> that even now, with twilight coming on,
> the spray the salmon casts against its death
> to give the stones a moment's gloss is gone
> —all in one unhurried human breath.

Like "Terminus," many in this collection are lyric poems. Their utterance is private, intimately shared. Yet the feeling, though strong, is played through the intellect, embedded in narrative and fact. Like "Terminus," many if not most of the poems in *A Vertical Mile* involve epiphanies, revelations within our ordinary lives. Secular though they are, they convey a sense of wonder, giving Wakefield's frequent theological metaphors their ironic truth, as we see in "The Age of Miracles."

Here we watch "Two gray-haired brothers" who have come to scatter their parents' ashes at the ocean beach where they all had vacationed decades before. Comically Wakefield underlines their challenge with echoes of Keats and Shakespeare: the brothers "stop to gaze/ at all that vast Pacific—cold they know"; "now barefoot they step out to make their brief/ but solemn obsequy, intent to cast/ their burden with no ostentatious grief." But if the waters have not parted before their feet, the "icy fire" on their bare legs performs another sort of miracle, for as these middle-aged men hurriedly empty their urns and "sprint for land,"

Four decades vanish with their dignity
until, two gasping boys, they reach dry sand.

Wakefield's poems reveal a passionate nature wedded to a critical
intelligence and a sense of humor. In "Signs and Wonders" we know
that the "shooting star"

it's grit
ignited by descent,
no message borne in it,
no purpose, nothing meant.
And yet we long to think
that moment's random fire
significant to link
our lives with something higher.

In a similar vein, "Petrarch," a sonnet named for an early master of
the form, reminds us of the costs involved in our realism. We know
that the Italian poet's idealized Laura was

flesh and bone
and no less fallen, no less stained than he—
and yet sometimes regret our jaundiced eyes
that taint the world and make us more alone
than one who was naïve enough to see.

"Holy Water" poses no such complication, but celebrates the miracle
of light that removes impediments as deftly as Moses parted the
waters of the sea. "Transfiguration" touches the heart of the mystery.
It tells of a girl who had watched her father paint the image of Jesus
that hangs in her Sunday school. She knew that this Jesus had "her
father's face," that the "holy glow/ was attic light"—that "in his
image he created Him."

And yet to her the painting was no less
a miracle, and maybe more. She saw
in it how we are blessed by what we bless
and made a part of what we hold in awe.

A recurrent pleasure of reading Wakefield is seeing how his sentences arrange themselves naturally yet inventively through his lines. "The Shape of the Year," for example takes us through the seasons from one winter to the next in a series of nine couplets that move from monometer to pentameter and back, all in a single sentence. Another shape poem (and how many have written these since George Herbert?) called "Writing About Love" tells why "Love is hard to write about." It does so in five rhymed couplets in which "love" or love—as the writer's subject or the thing itself—progresses, couplet by couplet, from the first to the last foot of his pentameter lines, not only making "love" the poem's first and last word, but leaving the poem visually balanced on the backbone of its theme. Yet, for all this artistry, the poem's statement is as natural and supple as its own final image.

The enjambment of sentences over many lines is a Wakefield specialty, but he also uses sentence breaks within a line to powerful effect, as at the close of "Crossing." In this poem a girl must choose her path of stepping-stones across a stream, the more direct route also requiring the greater risk. The poem's irregular rhyme scheme and varied line lengths reflect the girl's unsettled calculations, for

To keep
the shorter course she has to chance
an airborne instant, a heartbeat's loss
of certainty.

This crossing of a stream turns into crossings of another sort, significant moments of transition both for the girl and for the parents who

> . . . from the riverbank . . . watch
> and wonder what she'll choose. And what she should.

The punctuation within this final line accentuates the tact of the elders who recognize the limits of parental wisdom and simply wait to see what the girl will do.

Placed third in this volume, "Out, Out" is the first of Wakefield's titles to make overt literary allusions, soon to be joined by such others as *"In Medias Res,"* "The Waiting Rooms," "In the Garden," "Petrarch," and "If Music Be the Food of Love." Ranging from the Bible to Elizabeth Bishop, such borrowings accent the poet's originality. In "Out, Out", for example, he literalizes Shakespeare's "brief candle" but focuses not on its flame or the shadow it casts but on the "spiral of smoke" that rises from its "guttering wick," creating an image of ongoing life entwined with death—

> a filmy helix that bends
> through slow degrees to meet
> itself but forever fails to close
> the loop of fading heat.

Unlike the famous double helix it calls to mind, this twisting spiral is not a coming-together but a coming-apart, and the poem's second stanza, turning to the watcher of the candle, reminds us that even the windings of DNA have their pact with entropy and death. There

> Putting out his hand
> to snuff the last persistent spark
> he sees a once-black strand
> of hair turned smoky white
> that rises from his wrist, an arc
> against the dimming light.

And this book gives us so much more. There is the exquisite description of "Tree Wells," where mountain snows and evergreens create "cryptic runes in white on white" in a subtle tribute to Wallace Stevens. "In the Garden" presents a touching drama of marital love. There is the life we share with animals, domestic and wild, in "Contemplation," "Something Scrawled," "For All My Knowing," "Like Gods to the Machine," and "Things that Cannot Be Kept." These last two poems also convey a cultural criticism more pointed in "The Human Race," whose comically rhymed tercets are followed by the wry quatrains of "In a Multidenominational Cemetery." In "Old Words, New Context," Wakefield offers the grisly comedy of illicit lovers who, caught in an earthquake, are more concerned with shameful exposure than death, and through them the irony of a world that "sometimes creates a new/ context where suddenly all our lies are true." "If Music Be the Food of Love" includes this iambic rendering of a marital squabble overheard in a hotel dining room:

> It's *Do we have to go through this again?*
> and *Can't you let it rest for just one night?*
> and *You don't want to talk right now? Then when?*
> and *You're the one who always wants to fight.*

Throughout *A Vertical Mile,* as in this staccato repartee, Wakefield shows us much about ourselves and the various worlds we inhabit, often of our own making. What he reveals may be sobering or amusing, uplifting or distressing. But, carried by a voice as versatile as the intelligence behind it, it is sure to surprise and delight us as well.

—David Sanders
    Author of *A Divided Poet: Robert Frost, North of Boston, and the Drama of Disappearance*

CONTENTS

A Vertical Mile

The Age of Miracles

Two gray-haired brothers shuffle down a beach
they haven't seen in decades. Sandal-shod
like patriarchs they face the sea, and each
one bears an urn as if they seek a god
who dwells where breaker after breaker crashes
against the gull-shit whited rocks ahead.
But no. Each carries half their parents' ashes,
blended, as their mother asked, to spread
here where the four vacationed years ago.
They reach the water's edge and stop to gaze
at all that vast Pacific—cold, they know,
and waters do not part in latter days;
the age of miracles, they think, is past.
Now barefoot they step out to make their brief
but solemn obsequy, intent to cast
their burden with no ostentatious grief.
A dozen painful steps to stand mid-calf
in icy fire is all that they can brave,
and each upends his urn to strew his half
summarily, then flees before a wave.
The heartfelt words they planned are lost at sea
as with a new-found zeal they sprint for land.
Four decades vanish with their dignity
until, two gasping boys, they reach dry sand.

Crossing

The little girl has reached a standing place
midstream, alone.
Her bare feet arc to fit the stone.
She stands with slightly bended knees,
her arms held out, a moment's frozen grace.
She ponders her next stride
and sees
that one is an easy span,
the other a gap too wide
to clear without a leap.
But here's the thing: the rock she knows she can
attain lies slightly off the straighter way across.
To keep
the shorter course she has to chance
an airborne instant, a heartbeat's loss
of certainty.
She eyes the glittering expanse
of water, contracts her brows,
and squints to see
ahead to what next steps each choice allows.
She contemplates her complicated hopscotch
with all the poised solemnity of childhood
while from the riverbank the grownups watch
and wonder what she'll choose. And what she should.

Out, Out

A spiral of smoke ascends
from where the guttering wick still glows,
a filmy helix that bends
through slow degrees to meet
itself but forever fails to close
the loop of fading heat.

Putting out his hand
to snuff the last persistent spark
he sees a once-black strand
of hair turned smoky white
that rises from his wrist, an arc
against the dimming light.

A Scattering

That Friday all the valley came to fill
the church. Next day, alone, she bore the box
of ashes through their pasture, up the hill,
until she reached the outcrop where the rocks
and lack of water starved the few bleak blades
of grass that rooted there, a barren spot
where they had stood in spring and counted shades
of green across the valley—here a plot
of timothy, and over there a stand
of prime alfalfa, curves of cottonwood
and pine like verdant veins across the land,
then closer, where their barn and cabin stood
and all their small domestic traces were:
the garden laid in rows, the lawn new-mown.
The breeze that bore the scents of life to her
now bore his ashes, sown in stone.

A Second Scattering

Some bars of rusted angle iron, a sheet
of roofing steel, some fruit jars full of nails,
a broken power saw, a tractor seat:
a yard of things he found in yards at sales
that other widows held. He must have thought
each piece of scrap would prove to be a bit
of something whole, that all the parts he bought
would fall together in a perfect fit.
Now future widows waited in the sun
in cars and trucks along the gravel drive
while men in overalls came one by one
to bear it off. Their men. These men. Alive.
She watched the heaps of junk diminishing
as crumpled dollars filled her coffee can.
Could all this chaos make a useful thing?
Could scattered ashes make a living man?

Without a Word

At dawn today a coyote (say it right:
two syllables, accent on the first)
no doubt at the conclusion of his night
of delving into rabbit burrows burst
from tangled undergrowth, but when he heard
me tramping down the path he stopped and gazed
at me as if he sought the coyote word
to make me out as food or foe. He raised
his nose to catch my scent, more evidence
to help him place me in his lexicon.
But I was not in any important sense
to him a predator or prey, and on
two legs without potential as a mate.
If coyotes shrug away an unconcern
he did, and took up his unhurried gait.
A hundred yards away I saw him turn
his head to give a last, dismissive look,
then glide without a sound the way he came,
begrudging me the little time he took
to find that I was nothing he need name.

Facing Uncreation

A one-lane gravel road, a merciless grade,
the engine running hot—but where was there,
in all those endless Badlands, water? shade?
All sun-dried dust, eroded stone, and glare.
We stopped. What hope we had—it wasn't much—
was in the arid wind to dissipate
the heat that left the hood too hot to touch.
In sudden silence then we stood to wait.
Remember turning circles, seeing not
a speck of life, no fleck of green or blue
between the dim horizon and that spot
of stillness fate or chance had brought us to?
The deep and narrow gorges, gouged and grooved,
ran everywhere to nowhere, pointless, sharp,
as if the maker came but having moved
along confused left jagged scarp on scarp.
The silence flagged and we heard all around
a breath of wind across the measureless
expanse, a slough that could have been the sound
of spirit on the primal emptiness.
Did you feel then, as I did, something rise
inside yourself, beyond yourself, until
we equaled all creation size for size,
as if the void were given us to fill?

I'm asking what I haven't asked before,
because in narrow halls and darkened rooms
I feel *that* something rise in me once more
to fill another, vaster void that looms.

Spring, 1974

Our second-floor apartment window gave
a view of winding streets, a grassy park
where people strolled at dusk until a wave
of April rain swept in and brought the dark
more suddenly than usual for spring.
At that we thought the world was ours alone.
Our blinds left up, we saw the shimmering
and gleam of light as if on rain-wet stone
whenever parted clouds let through the moon.
Another squall to blast the glass with spray
then left a million moons like crystals strewn
against the depths of dark and shades of gray.
Now warm and in a half-asleep embrace
we dreamed our night of countless moons foretold
unnumbered nights for us in timeless space
apart from change, from loss, from dark, from cold.

Along the Weathered Bluff

All winter long, the thawing/freezing shears
great slabs and shards of rock from off this face
and leaves a rubbled scree along its base
to slow us trudging springtime mountaineers.
Now where last fall a weathered dull expanse
of granite rose we find an almost white
and quartz-flecked cliff reflecting southern light,
immersing us in double radiance.
And double warmth. We've walked this trail enough
to know that come some summer afternoon
the light and heat will seem more bane than boon,
though now, just now, beneath this dazzling bluff
I pause to lean against my open hand
and think this golden nimbus in which we walk
a sign of grace immutable as rock,
despite the shattered stone on which I stand.

Midnight Colloquy

Across the frosty fields some farmer's hound
is baying bloody murder, or at the moon,
or at a rabbit spore the frozen ground
has yielded up. He hasn't changed his tune
from hour to hour, to my untutored ear.
Of all our scattered souls there's none who pays
him any mind but me, I think, though here
and there another dog joins in to raise
a cacophonous chorus above the nearby farms.
And what's this sound and fury signify?
I listen hard to these confused alarms,
the curs' expostulation and reply,
a night's prolonged and pointless dialogue.
I wonder if there's nothing to express,
and if somehow this sleepless, mindless dog
is pointing to that greater pointlessness.

Holy Water

A long day's walking half again as far
as prudence would attempt had left him parched
and footsore, weary, when the evening star
appeared against the darking blue that arched
above the ragged Cascade crest ahead.
Now he heard the river, though concealed,
hiss and gurgle in its rocky bed,
but walled off from him by a boulder field.
His thirst was great but good sense held him back
from risking such a jumbled course by night.
He sheltered against a stone beside his pack
to wait for safer passage by morning light.
He slept, then was awakened into day
by a breeze as gentle as a breath and warm
across his face; and rising from the clay
he saw where stones were pushed aside to form
a perfect path—so obvious in the sun—
that darkness had obscured. At the sandy bank
he knelt and then, as eagerly as one
who'd never truly tasted water, drank.

Invasive Weeds

In clearcuts tansy ragwort finds a hold,
choking out the rich blue fireweed.
The tansy blooms a tainted, sickly gold
through late September; then it flings its seed
abroad to fields where sheep and cattle graze.
So come next spring amid the fieldgrass shoots
it sprouts, advancing in the longer days,
an immigrant who's come to put down roots.
It shoulders out the grass and taints the hay
until the livestock sicken, some to die.
The boy who spends a humid summer day
conscripted into weed patrol will sigh
with weariness and think a steer, a sheep
are no great boon to gain when weighed against
his sweat. He ponders how no borders keep
the tansy out, no pasture can be fenced
so well that something toxic can't creep through:
amid the green a yellow cast appears.
And what is true of weeds he'll find is true
in other fields he works in later years.

September Dust

In late September summer's dust has turned
a turbid pall on window glass, a grit
more fine than sand. Whatever dried or burned,
whatever died—the desiccated crow that bit
by bit the ants and beetles feasted on—
the season long has come to naught and slips
away, now scattered down the ways and gone,
apocalypse upon apocalypse,
too small if taken each alone to note.
The many nothings happen one by one
but burgeon into clouds, increasing mote
on mote to tint, to taint the morning sun.
It lingers on your tongue as if you've kissed
the bitter, gritty lips of Eucharist.

At the River

From Mary's Peak the valley's slow descent
to southward gave our river sweeping wide
meanders. Six or seven miles it went
to cover two or three, from side to side.
Around the stones and over fallen trees
I heard it breathe a languid vowel that fell
from snowfields, sounds suspended through the freeze
of winter, whispered now as if to tell
the secret cold to every lowland field.
Along the banks the trees in colonnade
traced out the vein of water they concealed.

On August evenings families sought the shade
to picnic there, and on the hottest nights
brought cots and strung their tents from lines between
the trees. I lay and watched their lantern lights
blink out upstream and down, then from unseen
encampments heard their voices droning low,
inhaled the scents of cattle, cedar, hay.
Beneath it all I heard the river flow,
forever saying what it had to say.

The farms where all the people lived are gone,
the people gone to graves—or town. The land
lies fallow. Yet the river murmurs on,
some days in words I almost understand.

The Sermon

The neighbor's crazy son got out
this morning, loose at five a.m.
He stood at Maltby's pond to shout
at browsing ducks, berating them,
as near as I could tell from bed,
for letting Jesus bleed and die
with mocking thorns upon his head.
The fleeing flock for all reply
quacked back in fowl cacophony.
"My Lord, my God, was crucified,"
he sobbed, and I looked out to see
him standing there, his arms spread wide.
His passion spent, he knelt in prayer.
His weeping mother came and drew
him gently to his feet, her hair
awry, her robe-hem wet with dew.
The graying sky was overcast.
The unreflective pond lay black.
The ducks, unmoved by what had passed,
one by one came skimming back.

Contemplation

The cat wakes up to see the spot of sun
that she's been basking in has eased away
across the kitchen floor, as it has done
a dozen times this silent winter day.
She contemplates the light from where she lies
as if she's weighing whether to remain
or if the work it takes to stretch, to rise,
to move is worth whatever warmth she'll gain.
And move she does, at last, to curl once more
upon the cat-sized circle, settled in
as if her little weight upon the floor
could pin the sun, could stop the planet's spin.
I'm chilled to think a prayer is but a plea
that God might deign to stop this whirling sphere,
to rearrange the universe for me
that I might have a moment's comfort here.
Then quietly, so not to wake the cat,
I rise and stretch, adjust the thermostat.

Fall of Forty-one

The war in Europe pushed the price of wheat
that fall of forty-one to giddy highs,
and when her husband showed her their balance sheet
the bottom line was only one surprise:
This money meant a new used truck. They'd pay
in cash, and pay off every cent they owed.
And as he'd promised her they'd do someday,
they'd build a warm, well-lit, indoor commode.
By winter they could do their business snug
inside, a corner of the mud porch walled,
the maze of piping plumbed, a cesspool dug,
the basin and the toilet both installed.
No tub and no hot water, and surely not
the gleaming porcelain they'd seen in town.
But no outhouse, no reeking chamber pot
for frigid weather after the sun went down.
And yes, it bothered her a bit to know
their boon befell them out of Europe's bane.
But would their traipsing out in blowing snow
bring back a soldier of the countless slain?
And thus they brought their privy safe inside,
and if it seemed like profit out of war,
the benefit could hardly be denied
compared to hardships they had borne before.

MRI

In elbow room, at least, this tube is tight
enough to be a casket. I repose,
eyes closed against the harsh unholy light,
yet sense a surface just above my nose,
a vast expanse of blankness I must face
but dare not stare at lest I lose my mind:
constrained, confined, constricted, cast in place.
Is this the darkness visible they find,
those hopeless damned who delve the underworld?
And then the noise, a pandemonium
of ripsaws, hammers, cries of sinners hurled
headlong to depths there's no redemption from.
I reassure myself this too shall pass
despite its creeping small eternity,
but in the name they name a nameless mass
I'll hear a final judgment passed on me.

The Age of Communication

On winter mornings children slouch their ways
from home to school along the icy walks.
They hold their faces downcast as they gaze
at blue-green screens. One texts, another talks,
absorbed, a distant town, another zone,
and some do things that these days pass for games—
but not with those they walk beside—alone.
Some watch movies squeezed to two-inch frames,
and all wear headsets planted in their ears.

It's old news, how an old man clucks his tongue
at what's become of kids in recent years,
how youth has lost its way since he was young.
But when I walk, the buses gone, I see
the frozen puddles last year's children cracked
and smashed like Vandals sacking Rome in glee
are undisturbed, the sheets of ice intact.

Signs and Wonders

That shooting star last night
inscribed its sudden arc,
an autograph of light,
and left a darker dark.
Men used to think such things
were signs of dawning ages,
perhaps the deaths of kings,
interpreted by sages.
But now we know it's grit
ignited by descent,
no message borne in it,
no purpose, nothing meant.
And yet we long to think
that moment's random fire
significant, to link
our lives with something higher.

The Sentinel

When he was nine or ten and long before
these million-dollar houses took the beach,
a gun emplacement, left there from the war,
stood sentinel above the water's reach.
They lived in a cramped and windtorn shack, its walls
worn gray as Puget Sound's oppressive swell—
the boy, his mother—and her rages, squalls
intense and sudden, impossible to foretell.
On days there was no school he left to walk
alone for hours along the gravel wrack,
miles to reach the house-sized concrete block,
and hours more to make himself turn back
along the sandy arc that he had traced,
the buffets loud as curses in his ears,
the footing loose and treacherous, the taste
of spray that wet his face as salt as tears.
On days the vicious wind from off the Sound
made turning back too hard to face he'd hide
there in a sheltered spot that he had found
long ago on the relic's leeward side.
That was where an iron ladder hung,
and though he'd come for shelter, something drew
him slowly upward, rung by rusty rung,
to where the unobstructed tempest blew.
He stood and strained to make his vision clear,
squinting hard against the stinging spray,
as if he might see trouble drawing near
and have some hope of turning it away.

The Naming of Names

You'd think she'd save her anger for the ones
who killed him, or blame, perhaps, those who sent
a twenty-two-year-old to face the guns.
But no. It was as if she thought he went
to get away from her, their unborn child,
and all the dreary years that lay ahead.
And how could she be ever reconciled
as she grew old and he stayed young—and dead?
Their boy was born the day, the very day
the telegram "with deepest sorrow" came.
It was a birth announcement, in a way:
Her parents made her give the boy his name.
They couldn't make her anger any less;
the name, for all of that, just made it worse.
The boy her parents said was sent to bless
the widow was to her a living curse,
and cursed, so any trait of his she saw
in him, the deep-set eyes, the curly hair,
and, later, the way he'd silently withdraw
from her, as if she wasn't really there,
was like the one who left was taking shape
before her eyes. And what the child had done
was nothing, but what he could do was escape.
And so she made the boy his father's son.

Floodplain

Through nineteen years in twenty, winter rains
create a muddy mess—though no disaster.
But when the stars get crossed the river gains
against the grassy levees, rising faster
than men can pile their sandbags rank on rank.
The water gets its way. It finds (or makes)
a breech and cuts its course across the bank
first here, then there, then everywhere. It breaks
the bounds that people hold as sacred law,
obscuring borders as the waters rise;
the lines of ownership that people draw
are something water doesn't recognize.
They say the earth was cleansed by Noah's flood,
the baptized world left laved in a holy glow—
no word of bloated corpses mired in mud,
a stench you'd think had wafted from below
the devil's privy, of splintered wreckage scattered
horizon-wide, of wedding portraits, clothes,
and bedding spewed through ruptured walls, bespattered
with filth and cackled at by gulls and crows.
Wiser heads who've seen a village drowned
know not to build along the riverside.
They seek the hills, but find that any ground
too high to flood is high enough to slide.

Finding, Leaving

No one walking in these woods would guess
they've taken back a town,
and quickly, in a hundred years or less,
unless by digging down
through duff he found a plank gone soft with rot,
a hasp grown stiff with rust
that once secured a door, so someone thought,
against—against—this dust?
These motes that catch the sunlight as they rise?
Against some nearer threat,
a gang of thieves, a neighbor's prying eyes?
Whatever. Leave it here,
along with what lies buried all around
among these evergreens,
and someone else in finding what you found
will ponder what it means.

This House, These Grounds

This house—the inside walls still bearing squares
of whiter white where photographs were tacked,
a missing step that makes the basement stairs
perilous, the landing window cracked,
the kitchen counter scorch-marked where it shows
that something hot was dropped, the bedroom doors
so warped that some won't open, some won't close,
and everywhere, walked thin, the softwood floors.
These grounds—the path completely overgrown,
the sagging gate, the pump arthritic with rust,
the orchard (apples, pears, and peaches) blown
into ungainly tangles with every gust,
and in the shed a tractor, stripped, its frame
the bruised red of wounds that never healed;
manure spreader, mower, and plough the same,
at intervals across the unmowed field.
If parting words were spoken, none remain;
a backward glance and then a shrug instead.
And yet an hour's looking makes it plain
that nothing ever really goes unsaid.

Orchard, Desert, River

The orchard smells of apples, mud, and sweat
as night comes on, and from a shadowed stoop
there wafts the smoke of someone's cigarette,
and from another the murmur of a group
of weary workers, rippling Spanish talk,
though in its current now and then he hears
an English word or phrase like a rock
amid the stream that babbles in his ears.
No one fears him, no one fears for him.
The boy is at an age between too young
to safely walk alone as the light grows dim
and old enough so those he walks among
might fear he's out for doing something wrong.
Those who notice him just nod, at ease,
recognizing the boy who all day long
works beside them in his uncle's trees.
A darker dark, the apple trees loom.
He has no goal but to escape the press
of humid air trapped in his single room
—and to indulge a nameless restlessness.
The desert starts where irrigation stops.
He crosses the border with a single stride.
The moon has cleared the distant mountain tops
and spreads its cool luminescence wide.
The scent of bitterbrush rides a swell
of dry desert air; he breathes it deep,

glad to leave the cloying apple smell.
Then suddenly the landscape tilts, a steep
descent to where the river runs below.
He stops to watch the winding river shine
and sparkle, elongating the full moon's glow,
the way the light and water intertwine.
He hears the sound of water over stones,
like human voices—and in fact he hears,
mingled with the water, human tones;
in confirmation a human form appears
from shadow, someone, no, two someones there,
two women, really girls, as young as he,
perhaps, bathing naked and unaware
there's anyone in all the dark to see.
The moonlight seems to sculpt them from the night;
their roundness molded to the moon's form.
Their flesh against the dark shows up as white
as frost but more substantial, alive and warm.

He's old enough to gaze without regret
or guilt but young enough to be afraid,
at least uneasy, vaguely seeing as yet
the change in him, the crossing he has made.

Farthest West

The men were sick of eating elk and dog.
Now having heard the Indians had beached
a whale nearby, they trekked through coastal fog
on narrow forest paths until they reached
an overlook: the sullen Pacific spread
in leaden gray, as if the fog oppressed
it with its weight. They named it Tillamook Head
and noted in the logbook, "Farthest west."
Below, half on the sand the carcass lay,
the arched ribs white, as seagulls swooped and cried.
Half-naked locals hacked and hauled away
great slabs of flesh out of the bloody tide.
They traded knives and bits of colored glass
for meat that Clark declared, at that night's feast,
was sweet as beef fed lush Kentucky grass,
thus wording farthest west by turning east.

Even the Disciples

Mark, Chapter 9

They left their boats and nets and followed Him
without a backward glance, forsaking all,
and not because a host of seraphim
directed them, but merely at His call.
They saw how He revived Jairus's daughter.
They saw how He restored a withered hand.
They saw Him calm the sea and walk on water
—and yet, and yet they did not understand.

There's comfort, then, for us who are unsure,
if those who climbed Mt. Hermon's slopes and saw
the Lord transfigured in a light as pure
as God's own vision, stumbling back in awe,
were still unsure, for all that they had seen,
just what this "rising from the dead" might mean.

The Heaven of the Senses

Whatever pleasure heaven brings to hand
I think it's texture that I'll miss.
What disembodied bliss compares to this:
the grain of wood, the grit of sand?

Of course there's hearing, sight and taste and smell:
breezes breathing in the eaves,
fallow fields going green,
the sour sweetness of a Gravenstein,
the autumn must of mired leaves.
But heaven, lacking touch, would feel like hell.

Transcendent endless bliss? It won't be much
compared to pressing skin to skin;
we find an earthbound heaven in
reciprocal indulgences of touch.

The Gods across the River

The gods your fathers served across the river
remain forsaken among the tumbled stones.
They gnaw the sacrificial heifer's bones;
against the wind, in rags, they crouch and shiver.
But worse than cold and hunger bedevils them.
They feel betrayed. Were they so hard to please?
Did one of all those minor gods condemn
a dalliance with other deities?
Now from among the ruins they see you raise
the temples your new, jealous God desires.
They hear you chant your psalms of servile praise;
they smell the savor of your altar fires.
And yet they know the perversity of your will.
They gather on the river bank, apart,
but sure no single God can long fulfill
the many chambers of the human heart.
They see the sidelong looks your sons and daughters
cast their way across the narrow waters.

Bumper Crop

The year that wheat was a bumper crop the price,
of course, hit record lows, and all our sweat
beside the roaring combines brought us twice
last year's tonnage—and double last year's debt.
One weary night as he brought the truck around
to take another load, my father said,
"There's forty miles of potholed road ahead
with dust enough to choke an Okie's hound."
What did I know of metaphors at nine?
The elevator stood two miles away,
each spring the county graded Section Line,
and what an Okie was I couldn't say.
The image of the dog, though, troubled me.
I watched a combine crawling slowly by
and pluming out behind it I could see
a looming cloud of dust against the sky.

Summer Night

Our valley held the sticky summer heat
and in my attic room I dozed and woke,
sweaty in the dark, to smell the sweet
new-cut alfalfa and someone's kitchen smoke.
With early dawn the air began to stir;
a cooler breath, still tentative and weak,
eased slowly down the slopes of Mary's Peak
where snow lay shaded under Douglas fir,
and then the limp white curtains swelled and parted,
my room grew cool, domestic valley scents
gave way to something strange and wild-hearted,
something high and cold, remote, immense.
And then I slept a sleep at last with dreams
of frost-split rocks that fretted icy streams.

Mountain Meadow, Summer

The air is calm up here today
but see, the wind has flagged the trees;
their twisted branches point away
from winter's bitter northerlies.
And if you squint you'll see the bark
is gnawed at twenty feet or so
above these flowers; that's the mark
that shows the height—or depth—of snow.
Whatever creatures live to feed
and feed to live up here make do
with little for their little need,
and sometimes less, the winter through.
The flowers nearly hide these blocks
and slabs of stone, split and tossed
from off those overhanging rocks
by alternating thaw and frost.

A day like this, you wouldn't guess
for flowers, trees, and azure skies
what winter is up here, unless
you read the scars with knowing eyes.

Successive Yellows

The carefully tended daffodils come first,
of course, but they don't count; their showy burst
of yellow seems too much a put-up show.
Leave the suburbs now and then and go
among unplanted plants that no one wants.
Invasive tansy takes a field and flaunts
itself above the pastures far from town
and flouts the county weed-inspector's frown.
It grows as fast as hapless farmers root
it up. A month, and other yellows shoot
skyward, Saint John's wort and goldenrod,
while monkey flowers and bird's-foot hug the sod.
The many yellows lie in layers weeks
on end through August, then the color peaks.
The tansy, first to bloom, is first to fade
and by September's just another shade
of brown. The celebrated leaves of fall
are all the colors then. The poets call
them red and gold, but pick one up, unfold
it flat against the dimming sun and hold
the last of summer's color, thin and frail,
and glimpse the remnant yellow, now grown pale.

Measuring Off the Emptiness

He strung the fencing wire from post to post
and squinted his eyes against the windblown dust.
He tried to see division as true creation:
The shapeless waste was given designation
as part and plat and parcel, section and township,
laid out in squares to match the survey map.
The void was given form as *yours,* as *mine,*
all parted and parsed by his wire dividing line.
Yet sand and dust were borne by vagrant wind
to cross and cross again, as if the thin
and legal line, so decisive to man, were drawn
in dust, and as they would when it was gone.
The wind would keep its ancient tenancy.
It teared his eyes with dust to make him see.

Things That Cannot Be Kept

The bulldozers come today to straighten the trail
from Cedar Lake along the wooded hillside.
Straightened, leveled, paved, it will be a wide
and efficient highway. The bulldozers will prevail,
don't doubt it, not we who have merely strolled
and sometimes stumbled like people with nothing more
important to do—because we are, and therefore
are ourselves merely obstructions in a world
that lives for fast arrivals, and damn the journey.
We put the woods to no use, none the law
would credit, no more than did the deer we saw
flicker through the shadow of tangled trees.
Let us hope the deer has already met
a death if not more kind then merely more
befitting its kind. Let it be gone before
the booming headlights come to stun and slay it.
Let it be gone before what we must accept.
The winding trail today becomes a road.
Some things cannot be stopped or even slowed.
Today we learn that some things can't be kept.

Even into the Light

Higher up than others dare to go
you find a cirque that holds a frozen lake
as if the ice age lingered there. To take
a tentative step or two is enough to know
it holds your weight. Another hundred strides
and you are at the center. You see that spring
and summer days are short and late in coming,
for the southern granite wall is high and hides
the lake (and you) in shadow. The ice will stay
preserved all summer, the lake solid and still.
There's something of the night that keeps its chill
untouched and even into the light of day.
To stand an afternoon at the frozen center
is to think the ice has come again forever.

Old Words, New Context

Think about an earthquake, the one that hasn't
come yet, and think of how there will be somewhere
illicit lovers lying spent and content
in a hotel room, pulses slowing, their
fingers entwined as if to cling awhile
to what they feel fading before the workaday
demands of life. They will try to continue to smile
to keep husband, wife, work, and home away
a moment more. When the shaking starts they'll wonder
if it's the aftershocks of their own passion,
if what they're hearing is the echoed thunder
of their throbbing hearts. Then the realization:
Earthquake! and each will feel the nauseous fear
that God has sent them a punishing cataclysm.
Each will pray, "God, don't let me die here
to be found naked in the rubble with her, with him!"
They won't die, exactly, but think of all they've said:
"This is bigger than both of us," and "It
just happened," and "My heart overruled my head,"
and "Against such force, what could I do but submit?"
Strange, how the world sometimes creates a new
context where suddenly all our lies come true.

Writing about Love

Love is hard to write about because
love moves. We're always looking where it was,
saying "love" and pointing to a spot
now void of love, now empty or, if not
empty, then echoing "love" as a cave will say
a name delayed. Or love is an image that will stay
a moment in the eye after our love has gone
into another room. Write "love" upon
a stick and throw it into a river, and "love"
moves no less fluidly than real love.

This Year's Revisions

This morning I walked the lower road and saw
this year's revisions to the abandoned place.
It looks as if an artist came to draw
in some things darker and others to erase.
New swirls of vines are scribbled across the faded
square of field, the lines of fence are all
obscured beneath the grass, the house is shaded
a pencil-gray beneath the lilac's scrawl.
But the apple trees are deeply etched, they bear
and drop their fruit. Two deer that smelled the sweet
aroma of apples were posed at breakfast there,
drawn across the fallen fence to eat.
The changes are subtle, taken year by year,
but I see the artist's intent is coming clear.

For All My Knowing

An elk. Across the path, blocking the trail.
A bull. And getting bigger the closer I got.
His grazing cows tightened into a knot
nearby, visibly nervous. But not the male.
There in the thinning morning fog he stood,
alert. Rippling haunches, shoulders, back;
the powerful neck, that wicked eight-point rack.
He claimed the cows, the path, the surrounding wood.
At twenty yards I stopped and thought what a blow,
one blow from a set of antlers like that could do
to a puny man. The wiser part of me knew
that elk are not aggressive. But did *he* know?
I turned, retraced my steps, glad to go
unharmed, knowing his reign would likely be done
forever soon enough; a chainsaw, a gun,
a road would come. *That* he didn't know.
I listened for his tread as I was going,
but he was content to let me walk away
—as my kind, I knew, was not to let him stay.
I felt no redeeming strength, for all my knowing.

Like Gods in the Machine

The cattle came running at their awkward trot
at the sound of our truck topping the rise, gears
grinding, engine whining, calling the steers
and cows to gather at the gate in a knot.
We stopped in swirling dust and climbed the load
and tossed the broken bales over the fence.
We were to them like gods come to dispense
communion, the hay a host that we bestowed.
They couldn't know how much like gods, to give
the stuff of life, but takers of life as well.
Surveying our supplicants we could foretell
the ones to be sacrificed, the ones to live.
Sometimes now I hear the rattle and shake
of something like that truck, and wonder who
or what is coming, what sustenance to strew
across the fence, what mortal culling to make.

Assorted Deadly Sins

It must be someone's job to clean this mess,
to sweep away the crumpled cans, the crushed
and soggy cigarette butts, the broken bottles,
deflated condoms, discarded vials and needles.
Someone ought to paint away the porno-
graphic stick figures copulating in acro-
batic contortions on the playground asphalt,
ought to sand away the four-letter words
gouged deep into the picnic tables and benches.
And here's a scattering of styrofoam packages
the crows and gulls have rummaged among
in search of morsels: taco, burger, pizza, fries.
Is it no one's job to get them out of sight?
This park is like the place I've learned I must
not visit late at night when sleep won't come,
a topology of thoughtlessness, accumulated
and accumulating in the dark, leavened
with outright wrongs deliberately denied.
Surely someone comes, sooner or later,
knowing how they'll overwhelm if left
to burgeon forever. Someone, surely someone.

In Medias Res

Let us imagine Adam walking out
in morning sun, the first morning sun.
Beneath that shady tree there grows, no doubt,
as if the world has not but just begun,
grass as lush as grows in the glimmering light,
for all the world as if yesterday
all the shaded spots of morning were bright
with late-day sun aslope the other way.
(We know there have been days preceding this,
five, in fact, but whether there were trees
and grass is hard to tell from Genesis:
theology is fraught with uncertainties.)
The river Adam walks beside has cut
its banks through strata never laid by flood;
now watch as Adam counts them, counting what
but years that never happened, recorded in mud
from which, we're told, arose our patriarch,
Adam, whose skull has suture marks that show
where pliable, newborn's bone was fused, the mark
of infancy that never was, we know.
Now take another searching look at all
those trees that must have growth rings deep inside,
recording centuries of getting tall
enough to cast their shady circles wide.
See Adam's idle fingers: Now they've scratched
his belly, strayed to find his umbilicus,

the scar of mortality where he was attached
to a mother who never was, unlike us
but like us, too, in being cast into
the middle of things, awakened in a place
with a past that we're invited to construe.
God creates us all *in medias res.*

A Hillside Pool in Summer

The railroad grade here cuts a mountain stream mid-
course, haphazard damming. There, uphill,
the forest runoff pools. It cannot rid
itself of winter's wet. The pool is still
despite the clatter-crash of passing trains
confused with purpose. Plumes of steam like sighs
arise from deep-accumulated rains
retained despite the warming summer skies.
All summer long the shaded contours weep
away the winter nights into this pool.
It spreads its darkened surface wide, grows deep
with unforgotten downpours. See, the cool
unblinking eye of winter gives the bright
reflected sun a shroud of winter night.

Triple Time

The old man, enfeebled by time's thieving hand,
is down at the bus stop. His cane helps him stand,
and glasses opaque as a mud puddle grace
the long scroll of wrinkles inscribed on his face.
The bus doesn't come, doesn't come, doesn't come.
At last he gives up and starts home with a stum-
ble. Watching him walk one maliciously thinks
what Oedipus answered when asked by the sphinx:
that Man is the creature that goes on all fours
at morning, on two legs at noon, then explores
his shrinking domain, somewhat less self-assured,
at sunset, requiring the help of a third.

Something Scrawled across a Field

I let the morning spirit lead
me where the headstones stand in rows
and I had knelt at one to read
if it was mine, when running, nose
to tail, a straining farm dog chased
a coyote through the nearby field.
Their paws in rapid passage traced
a hasty, cryptic script revealed
in green across the blank of frost.
The domestic dog was running hard
to catch the wild beast that crossed
the boundary of his master's yard,
and just ahead the coyote ran
with easy strides, his tail outstretched
to tease his cousin that nuzzled man
and sat and begged and heeled and fetched—
and maybe as well to lead him away
to where his wild brothers lurked.
Such turnabout would be fair play
in coyote terms, and might have worked,
but as a stone cut off my view
I stood, raised up by my desire
to see which would prevail of two
divided by the taming fire
of human hearths: the coyote heard
me stand and with a surge he sped

away, his ghostly outline blurred,
diffused in flight. The dog stopped dead.
We watched him: little, less, and gone.
His tracks were all he left. Appalled,
perhaps, the dog stood gazing on
the message that the coyote scrawled
across the field, growing dim
in morning sun, but something he
could read in words as clear to him
as what was on the stones to me.

Transfiguration

Her father's painting graced the vestibule.
The passing congregants would pause to gaze
at Jesus in the garden; the Sunday school
was brought to see how one who humbly prays
will gain God's guiding hand through any trial.
Blue veins embossed the savior's folded hands,
so real they seemed to pulse, though in a while
that blood would spill upon the arid sands
of Golgotha. The brow the priests decreed
be pierced by cruel thorns, so smooth and white,
immaculate but human, soon to bleed
for others' sins, seemed bathed in holy light.

She wondered that they failed to recognize
her father's face, for she had watched him stare
into a glass: his mouth, his nose, his eyes,
the look of resignation and despair
he'd given to the Lord. That holy glow
was attic light by which she watched him limn
the son of God. It was for her to know
that in his image he created Him.
And yet to her the painting was no less
a miracle, and maybe more. She saw
in it how we are blessed by what we bless
and made a part of what we hold in awe.

The Waiting Rooms

In pharmacies, physicians' waiting rooms,
and clinics where their viscera show on screens,
as silent as the scenes on ancient tombs,
they sit and stare at large-print magazines.
This is the generation that won the war.
Remember how the newsreels showed them then,
the women waving as they waited for
the ships that brought their virile, triumphant men?
And then they bore us, brought us up—and aged.
They fight a war of patience now, they sit
and wait, unlike that other war they waged,
until attrition brings an end to it.
But no. The waiting rooms remain the same,
still full, because by cruel calculus
the roll call comes up short another name,
and there's a vacant chair for one of us.

In the Garden

A week ago, at thirty-one degrees,
he saw the garden fenceposts etched in rime,
and now he's out here on his aching knees
to clear the winter weeds for planting time.
His wife told him this morning she would wait
for warmer days, as he laced up his boots,
but now the screen door slams, and now the gate,
and now she kneels among the vagrant shoots.
Like Adam, he can't help but think, and Eve
unable to resist the season's call,
except there needs no serpent to deceive
these innocents into a mortal fall.
He laughs; he knows the serpent's work is done:
his knees, his back, they feel like, well, like hell;
beside them both beneath this crescent sun
Mortality prepares his crop as well.
His laughter makes her ask, "What is it, dear?"
And he is suddenly aware he's cursed
to bear a paradox: this year, next year,
some year, one of them will be the first . . .
and selfishly he'd pray that it be he,
to save himself the grief of losing her,
except he knows how great her grief would be
in losing him. So which should he prefer?
He sees his hands grown gnarled and veined
with age, as all things mortal must,

and with his labor in the dirt now stained
and well along the way of dust to dust.
She gently prods his side and asks again.

(Is that the side where once, so long before
the snake, a rib was taken out?) And then
he says, "A passing fancy, nothing more."

To Make a River Run Uphill

A day of strong and steady April rain
in the mountains fell on eight feet of snow.
You see? Shattered concrete abutments remain
here and there along the river to show
where all the bridges from the Cascade crest
to the Columbia confluence washed away.
Families were divided, and yet felt blessed
—at first, at least—that no one drowned that day.
They stood on opposite banks to wave and smile.
The novelty wore off, and then they found
they did just fine apart, after a while,
without the galling constraints of common ground.
That summer a fire from a dropped match swept
from the confluence all the way up to the ridge.
You see those blackened snags? That's where it leapt
the river, to show that a fire needs no bridge.
Crops and stock, houses, barns, and fences—
everything the flood had failed to rout—
now windblown ash. Those twin pestilences
turned an exodus of families out.
A few remained to start again from scratch,
from less than scratch, and all aware no skill
or wit that man can grasp unburns a match
or makes a flooding river run uphill.

Petrarch

He saw a girl illuminated there
in April's burgeoning cathedral light,
and held the vision as an anchorite
devotes himself to one repeated prayer.
He never wavered, never let despair
or doubt obscure that single moment's sight
of something out of reach, enshrined in white
and real, yet insubstantial as the air.
We pride ourselves on being far more wise—
the woman, after all, was flesh and bone
and no less fallen, no less stained than he—
and yet sometimes regret our jaundiced eyes
that taint the world and make us more alone
than one who was naive enough to see.

An Open Road

The road to Honor Farm was smooth and wide,
graded and freshly graveled every spring.
When other roads around our countryside
were mired with mud, the prison trucks would bring
the chain gangs from the penitentiary
to labor days on end in cold and sleet;
when they looked up the toiling men would see
the trustees tending cattle, sowing wheat;
in turn, the trustees saw the men in chains.
A lesson for them all, and not so deep:
The road that ran between their two domains
was always open, always hard to keep.

Singled Out

This morning someone woke
to find his life has changed
forever at a stroke,
but not for good. Estranged
by chance, or fate, or God
from whom he was last night,
he lay there puzzled, awed,
distraught that something slight
as, say, an oncogene,
submicroscopic, thrust
him out of his routine.
It's criminal. Unjust.
He rose and dressed and sought
the self he knew but found
that every moment brought
another shock. He frowned
into the mirror to shave:
a death's-head grimaced back.
The morning paper gave
him names outlined in black
of those who'd been like him,
alive awhile, then not,
forever. Determined, grim,
he tried to put the thought
aside but had no luck.
He's singled out, he feels,

like someone lightning-struck,
and all of his appeals
go up unheard. And yet
tonight while changing clothes
for supper he'll forget
for just a moment, pose
before his mirror and see
himself alive, smooth-faced.
He'll knot his tie, then he
will feel a need for haste
to get somewhere—but where?
For some important date?
And then it's back: despair,
this sense of being late.

A Vertical Mile

A mile of altitude in mid-July
on sun-baked scree turns back the calendar:
up there it's spring. To make your way that high
means trudging ten, a dozen miles through fir
and hemlock stands, the air so thick with pitch
(though thin and growing thinner as you climb)
you're dizzy-drunk with it. You curse as switch-
backs turn you back to face yourself, and time
turns back as flowers, dead a mile below,
regain the yellows, blues, and reds of spring;
then swarms of blackflies, gone a month ago,
reborn to feast on you, each bite a sting
that says you're what they cannot live without.
Their buzzing fills your ears and turns your heart
to what you came here not to think about,
as if a place so far and so apart
were high enough to be above recall
as you continue your ascent to fall.

The Shape of the High Plains Wind

That wind could slam an upstairs door so hard
a stranger passing by would start and stop
to gaze in wonder across the hardpan yard,
then up, from sagging stoop to chimney top.
The long-unpainted siding and shattered glass
would tell the stranger it had been an age
since anyone lived there, and so he'd pass:
whatever slammed the door, it wasn't rage.
Or so the stranger thought. He couldn't know
that once upon a time within those walls
anger throbbed, crescendoed in a blow
the way our high plains wind brings storms and squalls.
Was our incessant wind somehow at fault?
Were those five souls inspired with malice by
its pummeling and pushing, the dusty assault
that brought an angry squint to every eye?
Or did their shouted curses shape the air
inside until, though all of them are gone,
scattered windward, their rage still echoes there,
the spirit of their anger living on?

The Human Race

Along the brightly lighted hall
the timid workers scurry all
the way all day to duty's call
that puts its prod to everyone,
so back and forth the workers run
on errands that are never done
entirely, for errands breed
more errands with such dizzy speed
that all the frantic runners need
to quite outrun themselves, yet fast
as they might run in panic past
their running selves they fear at last
they'll miss essential steps and fall
in reeling, mindless, helpless sprawl
and then be trampled in the hall.
And what of all this fatal haste?
Must life be ever faster-paced
until the human race is raced?
To one who were inquisitive
the lilies of the field could give
a lesson in the way to live.
But all the flowered fields are gone
to build more office buildings on
to house our morbid marathon.
Our race's pace accelerates.
But dead ahead, mapped by the fates,
another flowered field awaits.

In a Multidenominational Cemetery

This sunny-winter-morning frost
has doubly whited the upright stone
that rises in this overgrown
far corner of the graveyard, lost
to all but those who come, like me,
on solitary walks, or now
and then to trace an ancient bough
of some forgotten family tree.
Across the way the sun has found
the new-mown open field where late
arrivals lie beneath the weight
of markers flattened to the ground.
No upward aspiration there,
or none expressed in stone, at least,
as if the new-deceased have ceased
to hope they're going anywhere
but here. The newer fashion saves
in wages paid to those who mow
and trim the graveyard, row on row,
who care for graveyards, not for graves.
The chiseled prayers are all sincere;
they whisper to me on my walks,
but this place proves that money talks
so loudly even stones can hear.

The Shape of the Year

The sun
has run
its circuit round
and left us bound
in ice, though here and there
the frost-white buds declare
that spring will come by slow degrees
to warm the earth, beleaf the trees,
and then the languid days of summer come
with heather in a blue delirium
of bloom that seems to say the fall
is easy years away, but all
too soon the fields are brown,
the fiery leaves are down
and mired in mud
as if each bud
foretold
the cold.

Tree Wells

A nineteenth-century traveler's guide to the Cascade Mountains of the Pacific Northwest notes, "Particularly treacherous to winter travel are tree wells, the deep hollows around the trunks of evergreen trees that are formed as a result of the sheltering effect of the branches. Snow-shoers seeking cover beneath a tree can be easily trapped in them, and deaths have been reported."

A cedar sheds a winter storm
leaving hollow at its base
a vacant, inexpressive place
that takes the tree's inverted form.

The snow in easy avalanches
slides down boughs to make a mound
that circumscribes the tree around,
reaching even to the branches.

The breeze that bends from nearby cliffs
inspires the needled branch-tips pressed
like quills against a palimpsest
to scrawl in layered hieroglyphs.

It is as though someone has tried,
with cryptic runes in white on white,
revising endlessly, to write
about the emptiness inside.

If Music Be the Food of Love

The hotel dining room is nearly full
and unobtrusive Mozart plays just loud
enough to render unintelligible
the conversations floating through the crowd—

until I hear one couple's voices raised:
their obbligato floats above the rest.
The words aren't clear. I know the tune, though, phrased
and cadenced, not a nuance unexpressed.

It's *Do we have to go through this again?*
and *Can't you let it rest for just one night?*
and *You don't want to talk right now? Then when?*
and *You're the one who always has to fight!*

I dwell on this familiar strangers' talk
in strains too deeply felt to go unsung,
and notice Mozart's been replaced by rock,
the tunes we argued to when we were young.

It's their duet, but we could sing along.
You turn your eyes to mine. I look away
but hear a chilling turn in what you say:
"Oh sweetheart, listen! Isn't that our song?"

Last of Spring

On June the twenty-first, just after noon,
the sun shines down a city alleyway,
all other days occult and garbage-strewn
but briefly bathed in light this solstice day.

With endless labor ancient engineers
aligned their monuments to calculate
the holy turns and terminals of years
that no one comes here now to celebrate.

The year-around, though, warehouse workers use
their hour at lunch to shoot some hoops
among the gutters' green and greasy ooze,
the dented garbage cans, the grimy stoops.

Today they're playing in a different light,
a luminosity that gives their game
an unaccustomed lightness, almost flight,
and seems to set the concrete world aflame.

The shadows rise first waist- then shoulder-high;
the players' time grows short, they pass and run—
they spring beneath their narrow strip of sky
to catch the ball, as if to catch the sun.

Terminus

We end our climb and seek an outcrop's shade.
We gasp in mountain air, and every inch
was heartfelt effort spent against the grade.
Our pulses pound like lovers' in the clinch.

The stream we followed up its course
was full and fast; now shallow, nearly still,
in cool, clear pools so near its snowbound source,
too new, it seems, to know its way downhill.

Our sweat-stained shirts go dry. Our breathing slows.
A salmon flops and writhes, its long ascent
concluding where the water barely flows:
the fish's primal homing force is spent.

The gill slits stir up rapid clouds of silt,
then slow, then stop. The silver fades to gray
and disappears beneath a pall of milt.
The mountain sun has been so hot today

that even now, with twilight coming on,
the spray the salmon casts against its death
to give the stones a moment's gloss is gone
—all in one unhurried human breath.

Richard Wakefield, born in Renton, Washington, in 1952, earned his Ph.D. in American Literature at the University of Washington-Seattle with a dissertation on the poetry of Robert Frost. For nearly thirty years he has taught literature and composition at Tacoma Community College and the University of Washington-Tacoma. For over twenty-five years he has been a reviewer of fiction, literature, biography, and literary criticism for the *Seattle Times*. His collection of poetry, *East of Early Winters*, was published by the University of Evansville Press in 2006 and received the Richard Wilbur Award. His poem "Petrarch" won the 2010 Howard Nemerov Sonnet Award. His poetry, fiction, and criticism have appeared in the *Midwest Quarterly, Sewanee Review, Seattle Review, Atlanta Review, Light Quarterly, American Literature, Able Muse, Measure, The Formalist* and many others. He and his wife, Catherine, have been married thirty-nine years and have two grown daughters.

CPSIA information can be obtained at www.ICGtesting.com
Printed in the USA
LVOW060805290712

291982LV00003B/13/P